A Snowy Day

by Lola M. Schaefer

Consulting Editor: Gail Saunders-Smith, Ph.D.

Consultant: Chris S. Orr, Certified Consulting
Meteorologist, American Meteorological Society

Pebble Books

an imprint of Capstone Press
Mankato, Minnesota

Pebble Books are published by Capstone Press
818 North Willow Street, Mankato, Minnesota 56001
http://www.capstone-press.com

Library of Congress Cataloging-in-Publication Data
Schaefer, Lola M., 1950–
    A snowy day/by Lola M. Schaefer.
    p. cm.—(What kind of day is it?)
    Includes bibliographical references and index.
    Summary: Simple text and photographs depict a snowy day, including the
formation of snow and the actions of the people out in it.
    ISBN 0-7368-0405-6
    1. Snow—Juvenile literature. [1. Snow.] I. Title. II. Series.
QC926.37.S3   2000
551.55′5—dc21
                                                                99-18317
                                                                CIP

Note to Parents and Teachers

The series What Kind of Day Is It? supports national science
standards for units on basic features of the earth. The series also
shows that short-term weather conditions can change daily. This
book describes and illustrates what happens on a snowy day.
The photographs support emergent readers in understanding the
text. The repetition of words and phrases helps emergent readers
learn new words. This book also introduces emergent readers to
subject-specific vocabulary words, which are defined in the Words
to Know section. Emergent readers may need assistance to read
some words and to use the Table of Contents, Words to Know, Read
More, Internet Sites, and Index/Word List sections of the book.

Table of Contents

4

Today is a snowy day.

Snowflakes form in clouds.

8

Snowflakes fall from clouds.

Each snowflake has
a different pattern.

Snow covers everything
on a snowy day.

Snowplows clear roads on a snowy day.

Animals leave tracks
on a snowy day.

People go sledding
on a snowy day.

People build snowmen
on a snowy day.

Words to Know

pattern—a repeating order of colors, shapes, or figures; a snowflake has a repeating pattern of shapes; every snowflake has a different pattern.

sledding—to ride over snow or ice on a sled; a sled is a flat piece of plastic or other material; some sleds have wooden or metal runners.

snowflake—a very small piece of ice; a snowflake is made up of 2 to 200 ice crystals.

snowplow—a vehicle used to push snow off a road

tracks—marks left behind by a person or animal

Read More

Branley, Franklyn M. *Snow Is Falling.* Let's-Read-and-Find-Out Science. New York: HarperCollins, 1999.

Saunders-Smith, Gail. *Winter.* Seasons. Mankato, Minn.: Pebble Books, 1998.

Steele, Philip. *Snow and Ice.* Living with the Weather. Austin, Texas: Raintree Steck-Vaughn, 1998.

Internet Sites

How Do Snowflakes Form?
http://www.pa.msu.edu/sci_theatre/ask_st/100897.html

Snowflakes
http://www.macatawa.org/~oias/snowflak.htm

Snow Science
http://www.teelfamily.com/activities/snow/science.html

Index/Word List

Word Count: 54
Early-Intervention Level: 6

Editorial Credits
Martha E. H. Rustad, editor; Abby Bradford, Bradfordesign, Inc., cover designer; Heidi Schoof, photo researcher

Photo Credits
Index Stock Imagery, 18
John Shaw/TOM STACK & ASSOCIATES, 10
Photophile/Richard Cummins, 12
Richard Price/FPG International LLC, cover
Robert McCaw, 16
Root Resources/John Kohout, 8
Spencer Swanger/TOM STACK & ASSOCIATES, 4
Uniphoto, 1; Uniphoto/Caroline Wood, 20
Visuals Unlimited/Larry Blank, 6; Ned Therrien, 14